TWO WAYS OF THINKING

TWO
WAYS OF THINKING

BY

THE RIGHT HON.
LORD MACMILLAN
LL.D.

THE REDE LECTURE
DELIVERED BEFORE THE
UNIVERSITY OF CAMBRIDGE
9 MAY 1934

CAMBRIDGE
AT THE UNIVERSITY PRESS
1934

CAMBRIDGE
UNIVERSITY PRESS

University Printing House, Cambridge CB2 8BS, United Kingdom

Published in the United States of America by Cambridge University Press, New York

Cambridge University Press is part of the University of Cambridge.

It furthers the University's mission by disseminating knowledge in the pursuit of education, learning and research at the highest international levels of excellence.

www.cambridge.org
Information on this title: www.cambridge.org/9781107674004

© Cambridge University Press 1934

First published 1934
Re-issued 2014

A catalogue record for this publication is available from the British Library

ISBN 978-1-107-67400-4 Paperback

TWO WAYS OF THINKING

The eminent Chief Justice of the Common Pleas who is responsible for my presence here this afternoon directed that the lectures which bear his name should be devoted to humanity, logic and philosophy. So generous a field of choice even in the days of Henry VIII must have occasioned some difficulty to the lecturer in search of a suitable subject. To the lecturer of the present day the embarrassment of selection is immeasurably greater. I can only plead—and you will judge whether I make good my plea—that the subject I have chosen has at least some relation to all three of Sir Robert Rede's trinity of topics.

A well-known adage of the law pronounces a warning against the deceitfulness which lurks in generalities. Like many other warnings, it has more often proved an incitement than a deterrent, for the tendency to generalise is inveterate and every thinker has experienced its attraction. In sorting out the disordered data of experience, derived from our observation of the present and our study of the past, we are inevitably impelled to look for some general principles of discrimination to guide us in the process. So, undismayed by the attendant risks, I propose to discuss to-day a generalisation of the widest order, no less than the thesis that all human minds, in their ultimate assortment, fall into one or other of two classes or types, each characterised by a fundamentally different and distinctive way of thinking.

I am sensible of the audacity of one who, while not professing to be either a philosopher or a psychologist, yet ventures to air his theories on such a topic in this home of scientific learning. But, as Mr H. A. L. Fisher says in his charming biographical sketch of one of Cambridge's most distinguished scholars, "We are a nation of bold amateurs". These words, I need scarcely say, were not applied to F. W. Maitland, the subject of the biography, but to one who had temerariously challenged his accuracy. You will concede to me that the bold amateur may at least have his uses as a target for the expert's practice.

I have this further excuse—or perhaps it is an aggravation—that there is nothing really new in the broad classification which I offer you of the ways in which the human mind thinks. In truth it is as old as thought itself, for it is founded on the familiar distinction between the theoretical and the practical mind, between the study and the laboratory, between the Aristotelian and the Baconian, or, to put it in the language of the logician, between deduction and induction. But while I have thus nothing new to enunciate, I can at least put before you some verifications of this classical division and some reflections on its far-reaching significance in the world of affairs.

It was a personal experience in my own professional sphere which first made me realise the wide cleavage between the two types of mind of which I have spoken. It has been my fortune, after practising Scots law for a quarter of a century in the Parliament House in Edinburgh, to have found myself called upon during the past ten years to study and latterly to administer the entirely different system of the law of England. Superficially these two systems of law, except in a few important departments, have in modern times become to a large extent assimilated, owing to the constant inter-communication between the two nations and to the fact that for over two hundred years they have shared a legislature and an ultimate court of appeal in common. But I was not long in discovering how entirely different are the historical backgrounds of the English and the Scottish law. I found myself encountering the fundamental distinction between the methods of two of the greatest products of the human intellect which the world has ever seen, the Civil Law and the Common Law. In the contrast between these two famous systems there is evidenced, and nowhere better, the cardinal difference I am seeking to vouch, and for that reason I should like to dwell for a little on this topic.

When Justinian in his palace in Constantinople 1400 years ago enacted the Corpus Juris he promulgated to the world a systematic code of the whole law which was destined to be the basis of the modern continental codes of

Europe. Only the other day it came once again into its own in the land of its birth by Turkey's adoption of the Swiss Code, which is pre-eminently Roman in character. The most finished product which we owe to Justinian's inspiration is *The Institutes*, composed by Theophilus and Dorotheus under the direction of Tribonian and published in A.D. 533. "No law book", says Lord Mackenzie, "has been so much admired for its method and elegant precision and none has been so frequently printed, translated, imitated and commented on as the Institutes of Justinian." Indeed so early as 1701 a learned professor published a work on the Excessive Multitude of the Commentators on the Institutes. I am not concerned to discuss the success of Justinian's enterprise; it is the nature of his conception which I wish to emphasise. This consisted in the recognition that all human relationships could be assorted and rationalised in accordance with certain fundamental principles. From these principles the whole law could be deduced, and with the aid of these principles the law could be methodised and arranged. It is the conception of order, logic and reason in the regulation by law of human affairs. The influence of this conception has prevailed down to the present day in a large portion of the civilised world. Rome, in the words of the great French Chancellor D'Aguesseau, continued to rule by her reason long after she ceased to rule by her authority.

In England the process of legal development has been entirely different. No doubt in early times Roman law was studied in this country, both at Oxford, where Vacarius lectured in the twelfth century and incurred an injunction from King Stephen against teaching Roman law in England, and here at Cambridge, where a Regius Chair of Civil Law was established by Henry VIII. But although the Civil Law has survived in our Universities as a subject of academic study, there were potent causes at work which prevented it from becoming the law of England. I do not intend to pursue these causes so far as they were political, but I find in the failure of the Civil Law to establish itself in England highly significant testimony to the fact that the

English genius has always had a strong aversion from and distrust of theory and principle. In England a native growth of law more consonant with the national temperament and proclivities surely and steadily ousted what Wyclif called the "doubly alien" importation from Rome, till it came to be the fashion to disclaim any debt whatever on the part of the law of England to Roman law. In England the Common Law grew up out of practice. It was never promulgated as a complete system. It developed as occasion arose, for the Englishman prefers not to anticipate. "Sufficient unto the day is the evil thereof" is a text which has always appealed to him. The judges of England were said by Bentham to have made the Common Law as a man makes law for his dog —by waiting until he has done something wrong and then beating him for it. Thus the law of England was the product of the work of practitioners, not of professors, of practical men, not of philosophers. The famous system of the forms of action arose out of the necessities of pleading. You had no right unless you could find a writ for its enforcement. And writs were invented as they were required. In 1570 there were seventy varieties of them to embarrass the plaintiff's choice. It seems an odd idea that law should be what you can find a writ to fit, but it is eminently characteristic of the English disposition. Discussing the medieval law of England, Maitland observes that "Legal remedies, legal procedure, these are the all-important topics for the student. These being mastered, a knowledge of substantive law will come of itself. Not the nature of rights, but the nature of writs, must be his theme". Again to quote Wyclif—"The laws of England have only a few principles and leave the rest to the reasonableness of the wise". Such a system naturally lent itself to the development of the method of precedents. What had been done before should be done again. The question came to be "What did we do last time?" Not, "What would it be right to do this time?" And so grew up in England

> "...the lawless science of our law,
> That codeless myriad of precedent,
> That wilderness of single instances."

The two great systems of law which thus divide the civilised world between them, the system of Code Law and the system of Case Law, exemplify the two main types of mind, the type that searches for the principle and the type that proceeds on precedent. The two methods are the result of widely divergent temperaments. The formulation of principles with accuracy and precision is a peculiarly difficult task. It is much easier to appeal to previous experience. Constitutionally the Englishman has always in the practical affairs of life been suspicious, often rightly so, of the apostle of principles. If he does not roundly declare him a crank, he more politely terms him a doctrinaire. He has found that life is unconformable to any fixed theory and that principles always fail because they never seem to fit the case in hand, and so he prefers to leave theory and principles alone. Of that most typical of English statesmen, Lord Salisbury, his daughter tells us that his mind distrusted "large conceptions" in lawmaking as leading to the "sacrifice of realities to the symmetry of cherished theories". It was an Englishman who ventured to speak of us "Englishmen who never clean our slates", and it was another Englishman who described the law of England as an "ungodly jumble". But, says Sir Frederick Pollock, "being an illogical folk we do well enough on the whole with our anomalies". "I suppose"—again to quote Sir Frederick, for I am sure this sentence in that delightful book *The Etchingham Letters* came from his pen—"I suppose this is the only country in Europe where quite a large proportion of important affairs, from the Constitution downwards, are worked by just doing the thing you want and saying as little as possible about it even to yourself". *Solvitur ambulando* is the Englishman's motto and he might quote Seneca to justify the path he has chosen—*longum iter est per precepta, breve et efficax per exempla.* Thus the law of England exhibits what Lord Westbury calls "that distinctive peculiarity of the English mind—a love of precedent, of appealing to the authority of past examples rather than of indulging in abstract reasoning".

All this is constitutionally repugnant to the

continental disciples of the Civil Law. To them the principles of the law are what matters. The particular case must be decided not by invoking previous decisions but by logically subsuming it under the appropriate general proposition applicable to it. The principles of the law of torts, which in this country must be gathered from an innumerable series of decisions, are embodied for France in five brief articles of the Code Civile. Here we have the logical and the empirical methods in their most extreme contrast.

But let me bring my comparison and my contrast nearer home. It was, as I have said, my study of the legal systems of England and Scotland which first set me thinking on my present subject, and I venture to suggest that no better illustration could be found of the difference of mental outlook on which I am insisting than is afforded by the contrast between the legal history of England and that of Scotland. In the days when Scotland was first beginning to emerge from her rude and primitive beginnings, political and economic reasons alike directed her sons to the continent of Europe rather than across the border to the south in their search for education and enlightenment. The ancient alliance with France, close trading associations with the Netherlands and the fame of the Universities of Italy led to a constant migration of the aspiring youth of Scotland to the great law schools of Paris, Utrecht and Leyden, Bologna and Padua. There they found the Civil Law in the full tide of its renaissance. The philosophical system of jurisprudence taught in these and other great continental schools made a strong appeal to the natural proclivities of the Scottish students, who readily imbibed the tenets of the famous masters of the Civil Law. When they returned to practise and administer law in their own country they brought with them not only much of the substance of the Civil Law to make good the deficiencies of their native system but also the inspiration of its principles. It is not without significance that Viscount Stair, the father of Scottish jurisprudence, visited Holland twice in his earlier days and that it was to Holland that in 1682, the year after the publication of his famous

Institutions of the Law of Scotland, he fled for refuge and there found solace for his exile in the sympathetic atmosphere of Utrecht and Leyden. Stair's great treatise has no counterpart in England. In evidence of the spirit in which he undertook his task I may quote a sentence from the dedication of the *Institutions* to King Charles II. He proposes, he says, to offer to the view of the world the laws of the Scottish nation "in a Plain, Rational and Natural Method; in which Material Justice (the Common Law of the World) is in the first place orderly deduced from self evident Principles"; and he prides himself on the fact that "the nauseating burden of Citations are (*sic*), as much as can be, left out". It has been well said of "this comprehensive survey of legal relations common to all systems" that "the constant search after principles, the philosophical analysis and the thorough technical knowledge have given to a large part of his treatise a vitality and width of application unexampled, we think, among works of the same class".

I have dwelt at such length on the form of

intellectual activity exhibited in the evolution of the two great schools of law for the reason that the predilection on the one hand of the continental and the Scottish mind for the Code Law system and the predilection on the other hand of the English mind for the Case Law system serve to throw into relief the two ways of thinking of which these systems are the respective products. To proceed from principles to instances is the characteristic of the one school; to proceed from instances to principles—or perhaps not to proceed beyond instances—is the characteristic of the other. It is true that in Scotland the Courts now attach almost as much importance to precedents as do the English Courts, for the edges of distinction have been blurred by constant contacts; yet well on in the eighteenth century Erskine, the second of Scotland's great legal institutional writers, is found saying: "Decisions...though they bind the parties litigating, create no obligation on the judges to follow in the same track, if it shall appear to them contrary to law". He proceeds, however, to add that decisions "are frequently the occasion of establishing usages, which after they have gathered force by a sufficient length of time, must, from the tacit consent of the state, make part of our unwritten law". France has in the past resolutely rejected the principle of Case Law, but it is noticeable that even in that country there has been a tendency of recent years to resort to the authority of precedents, and lately there has appeared a volume of French leading cases collected by Professor Capitant, which may be regarded as almost a portent. To those who wish to pursue the study of the philosophy of precedents I cannot do better than commend a recent article by Professor Goodhart on "Precedent in English and Continental Law" in the January number of the *Law Quarterly Review*. One of the most acute criticisms which he makes of the precedent system is that it is really not entitled to the praise, commonly accorded to it, that it enables the law to benefit by growing experience, for, as he truly says, after the first precedent has been created it excludes experience. So it is a case of freedom not broadening, but narrowing, down from precedent to precedent. But, for your reassurance, you must also read the reply which Professor Goodhart has evoked, I must not say provoked, from the Vinerian Professor. Sir William Holdsworth will suffer no aspersions on the English method; he claims for it that it "keeps the law in touch with life and prevents much unprofitable speculation upon academic problems which serves only to illustrate the ingenuity of the speculator".

I hope I have not allowed my professional bias to lead me to over-elaborate the legal aspect of my thesis. I am indeed tempted to say that there has in the past been far too little appreciation of the law as a liberal science, too little recognition of its place in intellectual and social history as distinguished from its merely technical functions. A more enlightened view is gradually beginning to be taken of its human interest and, for myself, I confess that I find more and more significant the contribution which its study can make to the discussion and the solution of the problems of mental and social development.

Quitting the law, I proceed to pursue my

distinction between the logical and the empirical mind into other regions, and here again I find that the Tweed is an intellectual as well as a geographical boundary. The love of dialectic, degenerating, I fear, sometimes into an unattractive argumentativeness, permeated in former times the whole outlook of Scotland, religious, philosophical and political. There can be little doubt that this spirit was largely fostered in Scotland in the seventeenth and eighteenth centuries by the system of religion which then prevailed. Religious polemics were during this period the staple diet of the Scottish mind. While I was writing these sentences I happened to be reading Buckle's *History of Civilisation* and found that he had devoted a large part of his treatise to making my point for me. I am sufficiently imbued with the lawyer's respect for authority to be gratified rather than disconcerted by finding myself anticipated by that rather disagreeable author—no lawyer would say, *pereant male qui ante nos nostra dixerunt.* But I may as well demolish at once any claim to originality on my part by quoting a sentence or two from Buckle which I lighted upon when I had got so far in the preparation of this discourse. "Another circumstance", he says, "which operates on the intellectual progress of a nation is the method of investigation that its ablest men habitually employ. This method can only be one of two kinds; it must be either inductive or deductive. Each of these belongs to a different form of civilisation and is always accompanied by a different style of thought, particularly in regard to religion and science. These differences are of such immense importance that, until their laws are known, we cannot be said to understand the real history of past events"; and then he goes on, just as I have been doing, to find an instance of this divergence of method in the history of Scotland as compared with that of England. I would venture, however, to join issue with Buckle when he says that in Scotland men wasted their energies on religious polemics "without the least benefit either to themselves or to others". On the contrary, though I congratulate myself on not having lived in those times, I recognise how greatly Scotland is indebted for its robust and muscular intelligence and for its eager love of education to the intense interest which religious controversy engendered. I find Dicey testifying to the fact that it was "the popular discussion of theological problems in connection with church business" which, in combination with the high standard of education attained by the poorer classes in Scotland, "kept alive among Scottish farmers, labourers and workmen an aptitude for political affairs which was little, if at all, cultivated at any rate before the Reform Act of 1832 among the rural labourers of English parishes or the artisans of English cities".

No doubt Buckle's lengthy diatribe against the bigotry of the Scottish Church and its gloomy denunciations of all that is happy and beautiful is overdrawn, as is usually the case where the historian has a case to make, but the perusal of his painful pages does at least serve to show the undesirable results which ensue from the application of the logical method in the spiritual sphere. I have shown how the rational system of the Roman law made an irresistible appeal to the Scottish mind, undoubtedly to the great benefit of the nation. But when the same instinct demanded in turn that religion should be logical, the results were far from being equally beneficial. Again the Scotsman turned to the continent and found in Calvin's theology a system which seemed to promise the same precision and certainty in religion as the Civilians had offered in law. Hence the extraordinarily legalistic theory of religion which oppressed Scotland for generations. The Institutes of Calvin, a title itself reminiscent of his legal upbringing, became the Scottish textbook of theology as the Institutes of Justinian had become the model of their jurisprudence. Thus we find the whole relationship between God and man conceived in forensic terms. God is essentially a judge and lawgiver who administers a necessitarian code to which He is Himself subject. Predestination and election are the foundations of the Calvinistic edifice. Adopted as the basis of the Scottish Reformation, this teaching was developed with relentless logic by a people constitutionally disposed to legal formalism. The religious literature of the period is not pleasant reading, but it is instructive as indicating the extremes to which a ruthless logic may drive men's minds. Salvation becomes a legal transaction and the spiritual experiences of the soul are expressed in the language of the attorney's office. Covenants and bonds become the vehicles of religious conviction and testimony and the believer must subscribe to every article of a code more rigorous than any known to the secular law. Human nature must be regimented by inflexible rules deduced from *a priori* theological tenets. Such a view of man's duty and destiny may conduce to the formation of strong but not of lovely characters and its less happy fruits are intolerance and persecution. Extremes meet; the doctrines of the Church of Rome, deduced with scholastic completeness from infallible principles and as satisfying to the ecclesiastical conscience of the continent as the Civil Law was to its legal mind, found their counterpart in the rigour of the Scottish reformers whose minds had the same craving for infallibility and justified the cruelties of their persecutions by the same reasoning as the Inquisitors invoked.

It would of course be wrong to divide the world of thinkers on purely geographical or racial lines. There are no such exact frontiers in the intellectual sphere, and at different periods and in different places one or the other of the two types of thought may predominate. England had her own Puritan period. But while there may be temporary revulsions and sporadic variations, it remains true that the mental cleavage between the two ways of thinking is due to a deep-rooted racial difference, account for it how we may. The Puritan period in England was a phase of English thought when an element generally subordinate became predominant. But it did not endure because it was not truly English. Even Milton, in language almost reminiscent of Omar Khayyám, says that those who

"reasoned high
Of Providence, Foreknowledge, Will and Fate
Fixed fate, free will, foreknowledge absolute
...found no end, in wandering mazes lost".

The elements that make up the human mind are no doubt much the same the world over; but the proportions in which these elements exist among different peoples vary and racial differences of thought are due to the degree in which these various elements are predominant or subordinate.

Just as the Common Law is regarded as the most characteristic secular product of the English mind, the Church of England is its most characteristic religious product. What rendered it abhorrent to the logical Scottish reformers was its spirit of compromise, which we now recognise to be the source of its greatest strength. "The Church of England", again to quote the authors of *The Etchingham Letters*, "is the least dogmatic of churches in all things that can by any reasonable construction be considered not of the essence of a Christian commonwealth." "En religion comme en politique la souplesse britannique s'oppose à l'intransigeance romaine", says André Maurois, *à propos* of the Lambeth Conference in 1930.

But I must not tread further on these concealed embers. Let me illustrate the operation of the deductive mind in other perhaps less controversial spheres. Take Scottish Philosophy, for example. It has acquired the sobriquet of the Common Sense Philosophy through a popular misapprehension of the title of Reid's *Enquiry into the Human Mind on the Principles of Common Sense*, but in truth it is in no sense a pragmatic school. The metaphysic of Hume and Reid is essentially *a priori* and it is on that lofty plateau that they join issue, for Reid attacks the sceptical conclusions of Hume, not by Dr Johnson's eminently English answer to Berkeley, but by a rival technique based on deduction from different principles, in which to some extent he anticipated Kant. It is perhaps, however, in political economy that the deductive method in Scottish hands has yielded its most famous results. Adam Smith's great work *The Wealth of Nations* is essentially a deductive treatise; that is to say, it is based on certain fundamental principles which the author assumes to be inherent in human nature. These principles he then proceeds to develop and exemplify with admirable lucidity and from these principles he deduces the economics of human society. How far he was influenced in his method by his three years' sojourn and studies in France it is difficult to say. But while his method is deductive, there is no doubt that his work owed much of its success to the extraordinary variety of practical illustrations which he drew from history and from the world around him. Though never himself engaged in trade he consorted with the merchants of Glasgow who conjoined strong views on economic doctrine with conspicuous success in business. I find in Walter Bagehot's sketch of his life this passage which is so apt to my theme that I must quote it: "Probably", he says, "in consequence of the firm belief in a rigid theology and of the incessant discussion of its technical tenets there has long been, and there is still, in the south of Scotland a strong tendency to abstract argument quite unknown in England. Englishmen have been sometimes laughing at it and sometimes gravely criticising it for several generations: Mr Buckle wrote half a volume on it: Sydney Smith alleged that he heard a Scotch girl answer in a quadrille, 'But, my lord, as to what ye were saying as to love in the aibstract', and so on. Yet in spite both of ridicule and argument, the passion for doctrine is still strong in southern Scotland, and it will take many years to root it out. At Glasgow in Adam Smith's time it had no doubt very great influence". Mr Bagehot was evidently of opinion that the Scottish passion for doctrine was something to be rooted out, but let that pass. The point he makes is a sound one and we must include *The Wealth of Nations* among the other fruits which the deductive method of thought has yielded.

And so I might go on to trace in almost every sphere of the national life of Scotland the influence of this characteristic habit of thought and to contrast its products with those of the English mind. But it may perhaps be of more practical interest to consider how far the two ways of thinking enter into and affect the practical world of affairs in our own day. I have found it convenient to use, and doubtless to exaggerate, the contrasting mentalities north and south of the Tweed in order to bring into relief the difference between the two types of thought. But of course it is not a mere question of English and Scottish minds. Doubtless there are and have been many deductive minds in England and many inductive minds in Scotland. The difference is something much more fundamental and less localised, and my effort has been to show how pervasive it is throughout the whole history of human thought in all its departments. Indeed it permeates not only thought but action. Let me take an illustration from so unlikely a quarter as a very charming book which has just been published entitled *The Surrey Landscape*. The authors draw an interesting contrast between the ancient Pilgrims' Way which meanders in beauty through the county and the Roman road which traverses it with mathematical precision and directness. "The ancient Way", they say, "came into use naturally as early man followed the line of least resistance from settlement to settlement, but the Roman way was surveyed and made. This point illustrates the difference between the Latin and non-Latin approach to life. The Latin plans intellectually and dominates the scene with his roads and cities, his aqueducts and villas; they are, as it were, a pattern transferred from paper on to the earth. The non-Latin, on the other hand, allows his scheme to develop slowly in conformity with the natural features of the landscape and produces an irregular mosaic of curves which harmonize with the hills, woods and rivers."

Gratefully acknowledging this apt parable, I pass now to consider certain manifestations of the two ways of thinking which we find exhibited in the world around us. We all recognise the two types when we meet them, whatever be their provenance, and as a matter of expediency it is useful to know how to handle them. In public life every board and every committee contains examples of both orders of minds. How well we know the member who is a "stickler for principle" and who insists on arguing out each question on *a priori* lines, while the other and more practical members are trying to devise what is called "a way out". Then someone has the happy thought of proposing that without in any way detracting from their principles they should in the special circumstances of the case make a concession, on the distinct understanding that it must not form a precedent. And so the way out is found and everyone has the pleasant delusion that they have somehow or other contrived to make an exception without infringing their consistency.

In matters, however, of much graver moment than the conduct of our boards and committees it is worth while to study the tendencies to which the two ways of thinking give rise, for we have to deal with them in every walk of life and we encounter them not only in domestic affairs but even more in international discussions.

In the political world there have always been, and there always will be, two parties. By whatever names the rival schools of thought choose for the time being to designate themselves, the real dividing line is between the conservative and the progressive. I use these terms in no party sense but as indicative on the one hand of the type of mind which reverences the past, maintains the *status quo*, and requires the strictest proof of the need for any change, and on the other hand of the type of mind which has scant respect for the past, chafes at the *status quo* and is attracted by change for its own sake. There are no doubt progressive conservatives who recognise that the best means of conservation is a reasonable measure of reform; and there are no doubt reactionary radicals who adhere to their tenets with a diehard persistence long after experience has demonstrated that they are a clog rather than an aid to progress. The paradox of the conservative radicalism of Scotland was one of the most remarkable political phenomena of last century. I refrain from further instances; they may occur to you. But it remains essentially true that the politician inevitably finds himself on one or other side of the dividing line which I have drawn, according to the way of thinking which he has inherited or to which his temperament inclines him. I daresay that "Inductives" and "Deductives" would not make very popular party labels or afford very stimulating election slogans, but they would be more accurate than the designations commonly adopted. The inductive politician tends to support aristocatic government—which we are apt to forget means government by the best—for his class of mind relies on tradition and authority. He seeks the justification of his beliefs not in their logic or their conformity to any predetermined principles, but in experience. Like the followers of the Common Law he believes in precedents. The deductive politician on the other hand tends to support democracy. He derides as unscientific the system of hereditary government, he is impatient with the abuses and imperfections of the illogical present; and, having adopted certain *a priori* doctrines of the equality and perfectibility of man, he seeks to shape the ends of society to his theories. Again my analogy holds; he is a follower of the Civilians and believes in principles. But in this country of England even the most radically minded are themselves subject to the *genius loci*. As England preferred to work out her own legal salvation in her Common Law, so in her politics all parties, even the most advanced, have tended to exhibit a certain practical good sense, a reluctance to push things to their logical extremes. The French Revolution affords the most dramatic example in history of logic applied to government—or did, until Russia afforded us a more modern instance. These two great experiments alike illustrate the working of the deductive mind. "The commonplaces of politics in France", says John Stuart Mill, "are large and sweeping practical maxims from which, as ultimate premisses, men reason downwards to particular applications, and this they call being logical and consistent. For instance, they are perpetually arguing that such and such a measure ought to be adopted because it is a consequence of the principle on which the form of government is founded; of the principle of legitimacy or the principle of the sovereignty of the people." Certain principles are assumed as axiomatic and then all the rest follows.

It has been said that the politics of this country in the past century were dominated by the revulsion of feeling occasioned by the object lesson of the French Revolution, perhaps even more that of 1848 than that of 1789. While the excesses of our neighbours across the Channel were doubtless used to point a political moral, they did not create, though they may well have strengthened, the natural instinct of the people of England to distrust new-fangled theories imported from abroad. The matter is so admirably put by Lord Morley, to whom I am also indebted for my quotation from Mill, that I must give the passage in full. "The influence", he says, "of France upon England since the revolution of 1848 has tended wholly to the discredit of abstract theory and general reasoning among us, in all that relates to politics, morals and religion. In 1848, not in 1789, questions affecting the fundamental structure and organic condition of the social union came for the first time into formidable prominence. For the first time these questions and the answers to them were stated in articulate formulas and distinct theories." These "premature attempts to convert a crude aspiration into a political reality and to found a new social order on a number of uncompromising deductions from

abstract principles of the common weal...
have had the natural effect of deepening the
English dislike of a general theory even when
such a theory did no more than profess to
announce a remote object of desire and not
the present goal of immediate effort".

I doubt if we sufficiently appreciate the
totally different approach which the continental, and particularly the Latin, mind makes
to every problem as contrasted with what I
may call the British approach. It needs imagination to enter into another mentality and
imagination is not the strong suit of the
English race. "The power of realising and
understanding types of character very different from our own is not, I think, an English
quality", says Lecky in his discourse on
The Political Value of History. I believe that
the failure of the multitude of international
conferences of recent years to achieve the
aims which we all profess to have in common
is in no small degree due to the incompati-
bility of the ways of thinking of those who
have participated in them. That at least is the
view, I gather, which is held by one of the

most acute of French observers, who has the advantage of an unusually sympathetic comprehension of the British temperament. In *Mes Songes que Voici*, from which I have already quoted, M. André Maurois confides to us, in a passage of remarkable insight, how he sees the two types of mind at work. "De Rome", he says, "et peut-être aussi d'une longue vie paysanne, la France tient le goût de l'exactitude juridique, des formules, et des textes précis. L'Angleterre mène sa vie politique sans constitution, rend la justice sans code et attend la paix de l'Europe d'expédients contradictoires et d'intuitions hardies. La France veut des chartes écrites et des garanties signées. L'Anglais tient pour dangereux de prétendre endiguer un univers aux crues imprévisables. Le Français croit aux plans, aux édifices symétriques, aux desseins fermes et bien conçus. L'Anglais, s'il rencontre une résistance doctrinale, semble céder, puis revient à la charge dans une autre formation et reprend le terrain perdu. Obligé de concéder à un pays son indépendance, il reconnaît l'indépendance et maintient l'occupation. Un Français eût maintenu le principe au risque de perdre le gage. De tels contrastes entre les idéologies nationales naissent les malentendus qui, depuis la guerre, ont rendu difficile la vie de l'Europe."

My discerning hearers will have observed that M. Maurois finds, as I have done, that it is the same British instinct which expresses itself in "la justice sans code" that animates the British mind in dealing with international affairs, just as it is France's inheritance from Rome which influences her in her very different attitude. I am, again, fortunate in having my point so felicitously made for me.

Professor Graham Wallas has collected for us, in his *Art of Thought*, an interesting anthology of English and French pronouncements on the differing mentalities of the English and the French politician. He declines to accept the common attribution of the difference to racial biology and states it as his own belief that it is "mainly due to a difference of intellectual tradition, transmitted partly by education and partly by political catchwords and legal institutions and strengthened by differences in the political and international history of the two countries". I cannot say that I find this very satisfying but there I must leave it.

Hitherto, as you will have observed, I have confined myself to the exposition and illustration of the two ways of thinking and have sedulously refrained from expressing any opinion upon their relative merits. Perhaps I should be wise to close without doing so, but the temptation to appraise is difficult to resist. If we are to judge by results, by the test of which kind of mind attains the greatest measure of practical success in the art of government and so best promotes human welfare, I am disposed to award the palm to the inductive mind as exemplified in the English race. I speak as a Scotsman whose national and hereditary proclivities may sometimes render him a little critical of the Englishman's way of working out his problems. The Englishman's spirit of opportunism and compromise may sometimes exasperate his logical neighbours across the border and on the continent, but we owe to them Magna Charta and the British Empire. Let me quote the tribute of General Alexandre, one of Joffre's staff-officers, who in the Great War experienced the difficulty of comprehending the English mind. After dwelling on the English habit of refusing to look ahead, of troubling only about the affairs of the current day, of waiting for the event to happen in order to deal with it, he concludes: "Has not the history of a thousand years proved that this manner of doing things has overcome temporary set-backs and has always led to final success".

I recall a conversation I once had with a very eminent continental diplomatist who startled me by declaring that the English were the most revolutionary nation in the world; but then he added that we never noticed that our revolutions were taking place. There is truth in this. Unlike the more spectacular revolutions of other nations, ours are not effected either by syllogisms or machine guns but by gradual and almost imperceptible pro-cesses of change and for that very reason are more fundamental and permanent. It is a merit of our characteristically unwritten constitution that great social alterations can be brought about without destroying the framework of our body politic, and without our ever quite realising what is happening or sustaining the shocks which such changes would give to a more rigid structure. A written constitution compels the revolutionary to face the logic of his policy; an unwritten constitution enables him to avoid it. This again is a source of strength for it prevents much wasteful conflict, but it is exasperating to the theorist.

When all is said and done, it is the tolerance, the magnanimity, the readiness to compromise and to assimilate, the very illogicality, if you will, that are so typical of the English mind which have always been the secret of England's influence and power and which at this moment, when the whole of the rest of the world is seething with new theories of government, new theories of economics, new theories of everything, have enabled her to retain a stability which is the envy of every other nation.

But it may be said that I am applying too

utilitarian a test of excellence. Can it be said that a higher ethical value can be assigned to the one type of mind than to the other? Here I find my theme in danger of soaring into the region of the ultimate antinomy between Reason and Authority. In the present day these ancient adversaries once more confront each other, but each is a little less self-confident than it used to be. It is less easy nowadays to be either a convinced rationalist or an impenetrable authoritarian. We are all a little less sure of our ground, a little less supercilious in the assertion of our dogmas. When our most eminent scientists demonstrate the relativity of the laws which their predecessors regarded as absolute, the common man may well wonder where he stands. Intellectually, the recent spectacular developments of science have, oddly enough, engendered a new humility in their exponents, while the mandarins of authority have grown more modest in the assertion of their creeds, as so many of the articles of their faith have been shattered by the world's upheaval. All this is of good augury, for the true answer to the problem I have stated as to the comparative value to mankind of the two ways of thinking is that there is no answer. Neither method is intellectually or ethically better than the other. Both are essential. At different times and in different places, in one race or in another, sometimes the one habit of mind and sometimes the other is found to predominate, lending its distinctive colour, variety and interest to thought and practice, but the world has need of both ways of thinking. Each has its contribution to make to the attainment of the goal of all right ways of thinking—the Truth.

www.ingramcontent.com/pod-product-compliance
Ingram Content Group UK Ltd.
Pitfield, Milton Keynes, MK11 3LW, UK
UKHW042141280225
455719UK00001B/15